McGrath Math

TEDDY BEAR
SUBTRACTION

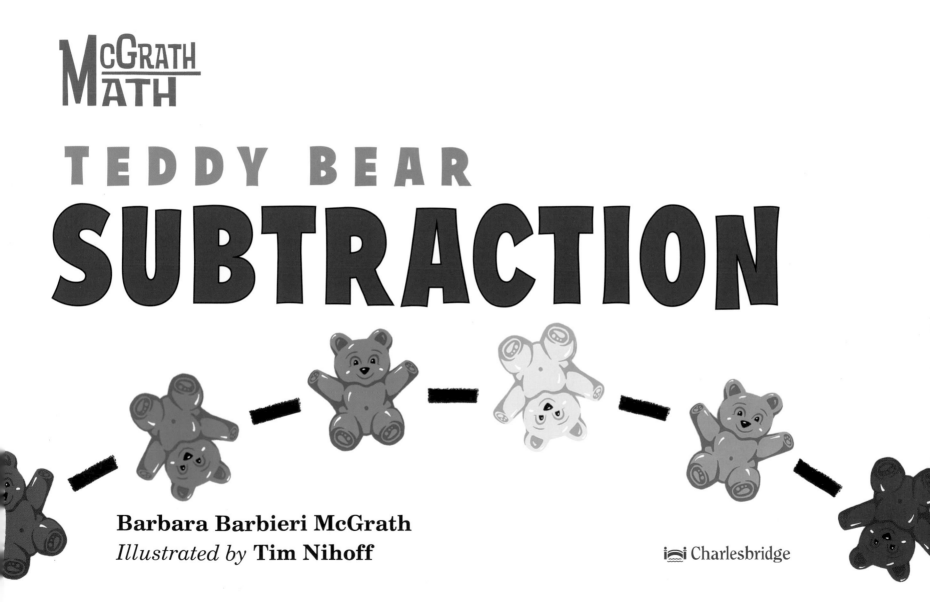

Barbara Barbieri McGrath
Illustrated by **Tim Nihoff**

Charlesbridge

With love to Vaughn A.—B. B. M.

To Whitney, my sweet teddy-bear sister—T. N.

Text copyright © 2016 by Barbara Barbieri McGrath
Illustrations copyright © 2016 by Tim Nihoff

Published by Charlesbridge
85 Main Street, Watertown, MA 02472
(617) 926-0329 • www.charlesbridge.com

Illustrations hand drawn digitally and collaged with
    found objects in Adobe Photoshop
Display type set in Animated Gothic by BA Graphics
Text type set in Century Schoolbook by Monotype
Equations type set in Billy by SparkyType
Color separations by Colourscan Print Co Pte Ltd, Singapore
Printed by Jade Productions in Heyuan, Guangdong, China
Production supervision by Brian G. Walker
Designed by Whitney Leader-Picone and Diane M. Earley

Library of Congress Cataloging-in-Publication Data
McGrath, Barbara Barbieri, 1954- author.
    Teddy bear subtraction / Barbara Barbieri McGrath;
illustrated by Tim Nihoff.
        pages cm
    ISBN 978-1-58089-426-5 (reinforced for library use)
    ISBN 978-1-58089-427-2 (softcover)
    ISBN 978-1-60734-792-7 (ebook)
    ISBN 978-1-60734-652-4 (ebook PDF)
1. Subtraction—Juvenile literature. 2. Counting—Juvenile
literature. I. Nihoff, Tim, illustrator. II. Title.

QA115.M389 2015
513.2'12—dc23   2013014224

Printed in China
(hc) 10 9 8 7 6 5 4 3 2 1
(sc) 10 9 8 7 6 5 4 3 2 1

Teddies are ready—
they're bustling about.
It's time to subtract.
Won't you help them out?

If you have a group of teddies, and a number of the teddies walk away from the group, they are being subtracted.

Let's get the bears ready.
Sort by color, please.
Call each group a set.
It's really a breeze.

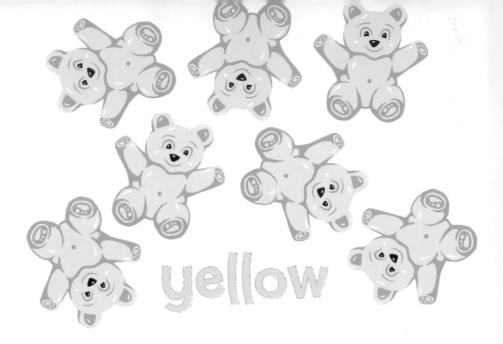

yellow

blue

purple

orange

green

Spread out the bears.
Sort them so that you have
six groups of different colors.
Each group is called a set.

red

Before teddies subtract,
you must count, count, count.
Just how many bears
make up the total amount?

7

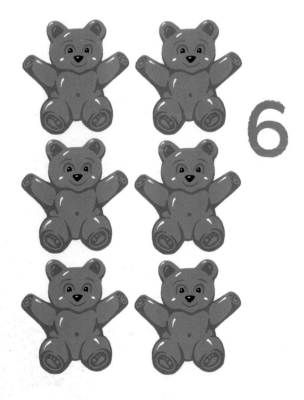

6

3

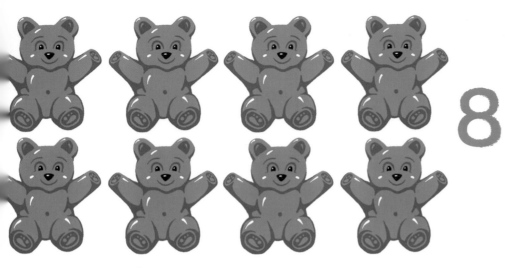

8

4

12

When you add up the teddies, there are forty in all!

It's fun to compare.
No set is the same.
Which set has less?
Let's make it a game.

When it's time to subtract, you'll take away a smaller amount of teddies from a bigger amount of teddies. First, find out which color set has more teddies and which has fewer.

3 < 6   The "less than" sign

<

purple < blue

Three is less than six.

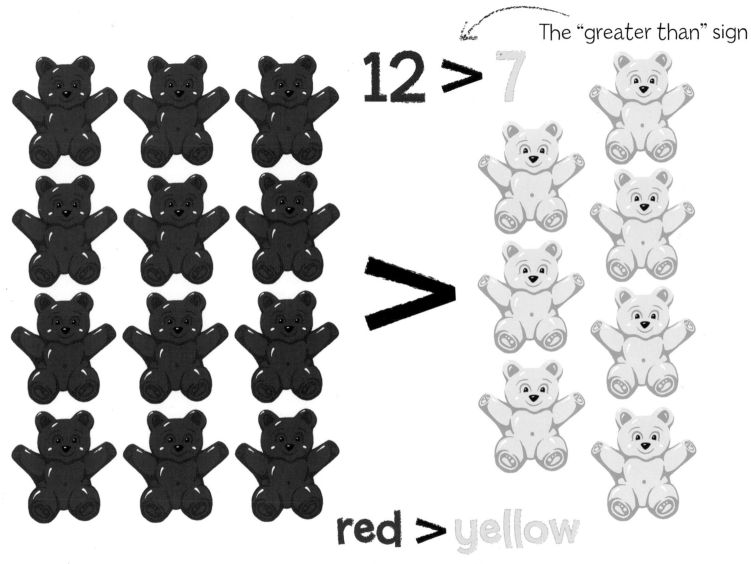

The "greater than" sign

12 > 7

red > yellow

Twelve is more than seven.

It's time to subtract.
It's easy, you'll see.
Take two teddies away—
what will the answer be?

Start with a set of six teddies.
Six is the bigger number in the
equation. Take two teddies away from
the set. Two is the smaller number. The
bigger number goes first. The smaller
number follows the minus sign.
The answer is called the difference.
It comes after the equal sign.

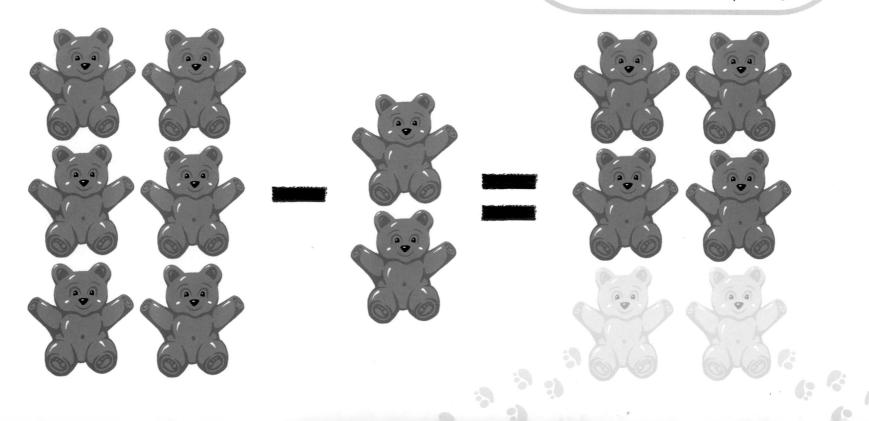

An equation is a number sentence. Let's try writing one.

bigger number (**minuend**)

smaller number (**subtrahend**)

the **difference** between the two numbers

6 - 2 = 4

minus sign

equal sign

You say the equation like this:
Six minus two equals four.

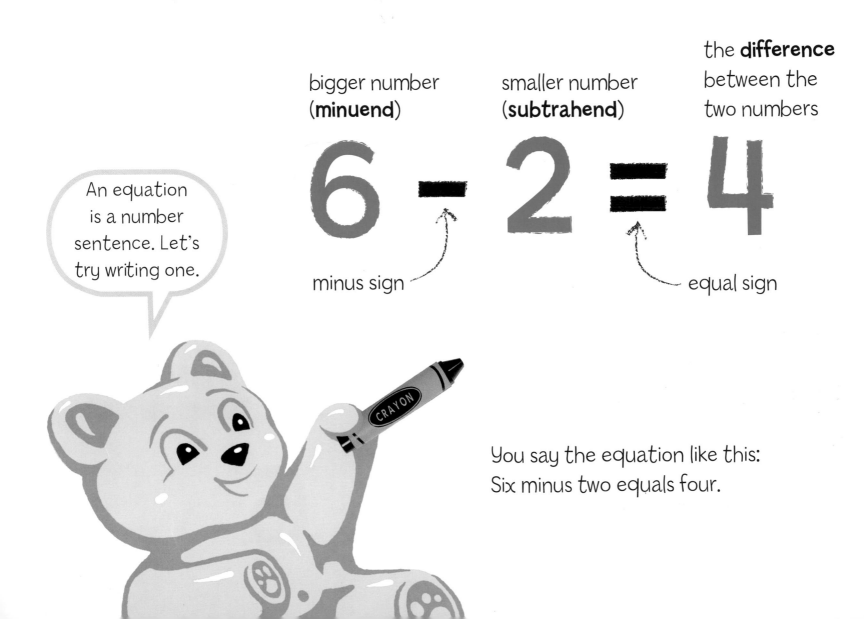

Equations are handy!
See how they explain
how many to remove
and how many remain.

$$8 - 2 = 6$$

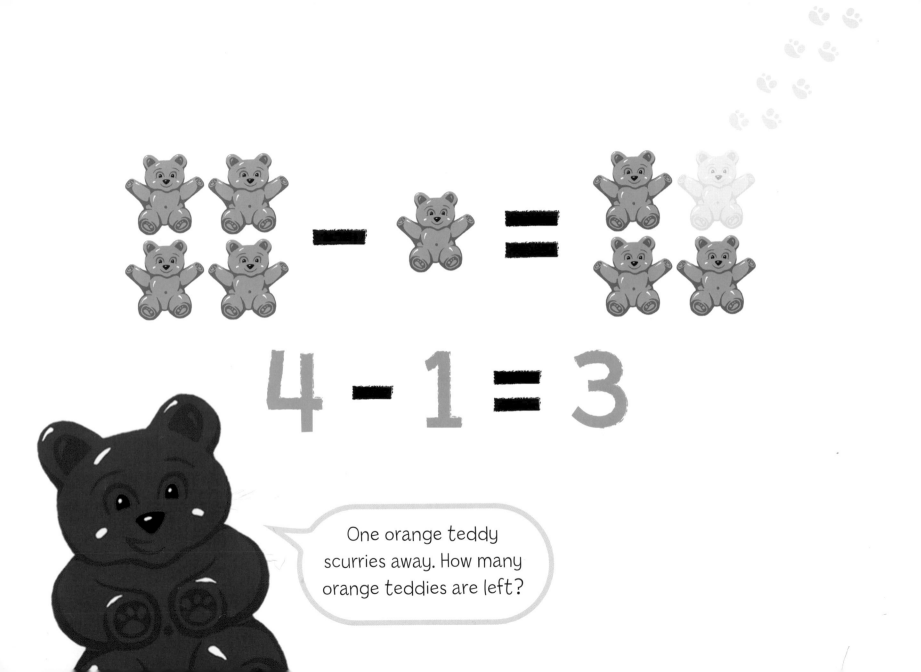

Bears keep subtracting!
What's left at the end
when the teddies say
so long to a friend?

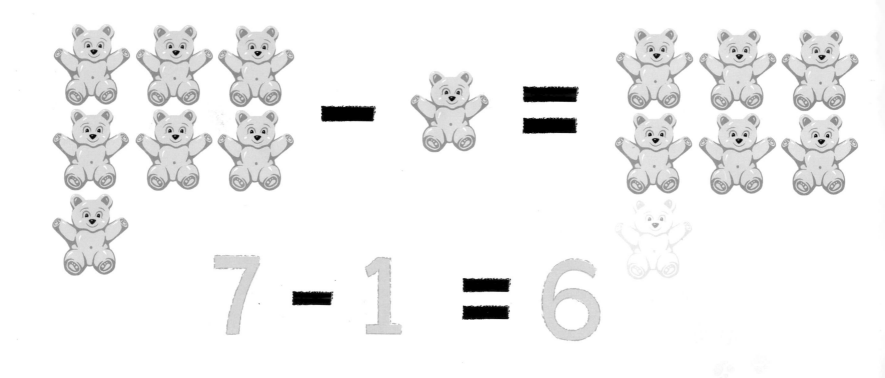

3 - 1 = 2

Teddies love to play.
It's so hard to stop!
We'll now try subtracting
with the big number on top.

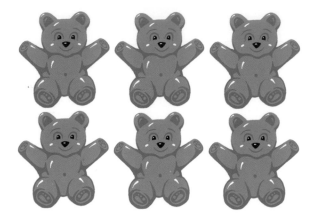

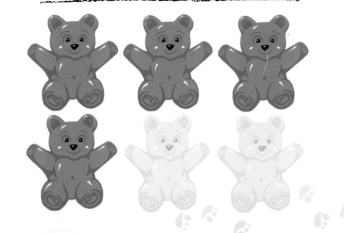

6 bigger number on top (**minuend**)

minus sign

- 2 smaller number under (**subtrahend**)

equal sign

4 **difference** on the bottom

Let's set up the subtraction problem in a different way! Remember, when subtracting a number greater than zero, the answer is always less than the number you subtracted from.

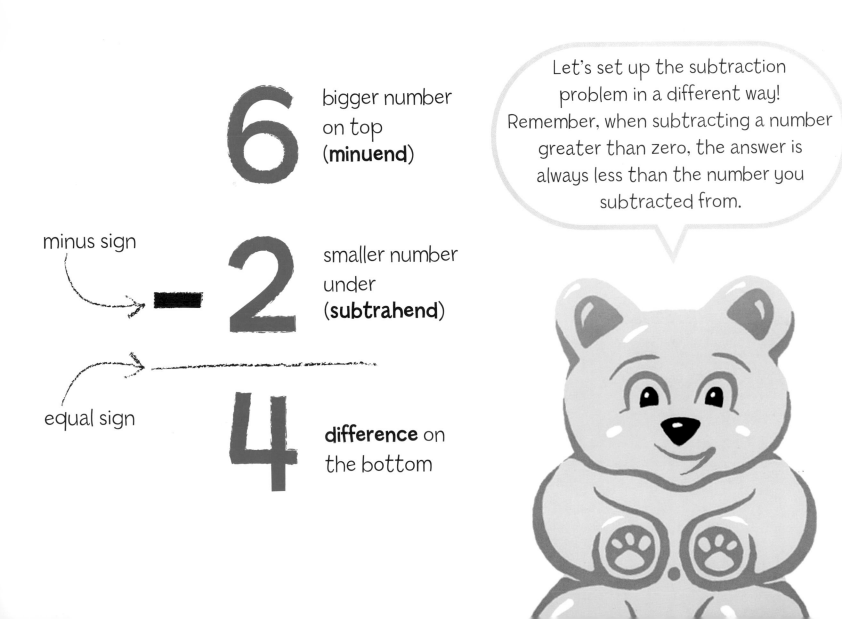

More teddy equations?
What do you say?

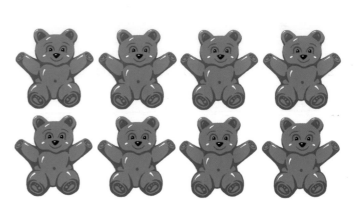

The bottom from the top
is what you take away.

$$12$$
$$-\ 5$$
$$\overline{}$$
$$7$$

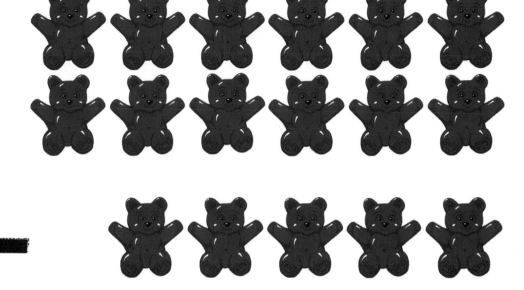

−

Subtracting starts with
the total you once had.

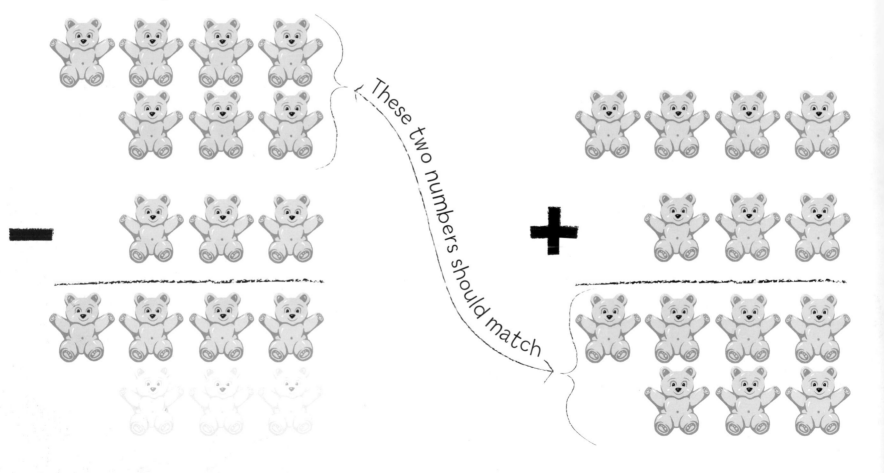

These two numbers should match

To check your answer,
you just have to add.

The opposite of subtraction is addition. It's always a good idea to check your answer. In subtraction—it's easy—just add your answer to the number you took away. Does that add up to the number you started with? Then you did it right!

7
- 3
———
4

These two numbers should match

4
+ 3
———
7

CRAYON

To subtract large numbers,
it's important to see
that digits, values,
and columns are key.

Digits

0 1 2 3 4 5 6 7 8 9

The numbers 0 through 9 are called digits.

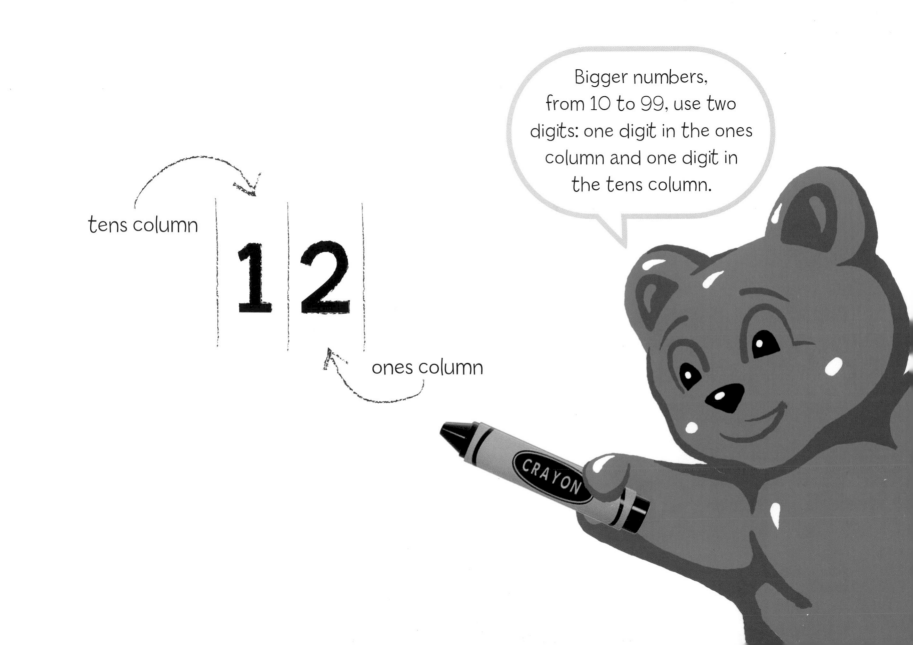

Now subtract the teddies—
they want to have fun.

Wow—your answer has two digits, not one!

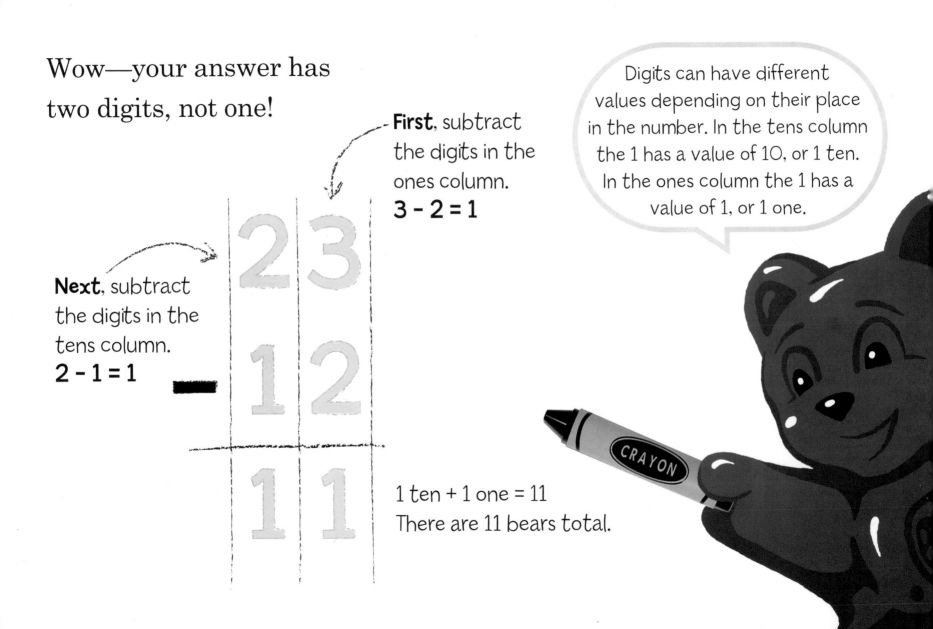

First, subtract the digits in the ones column.
3 - 2 = 1

Digits can have different values depending on their place in the number. In the tens column the 1 has a value of 10, or 1 ten. In the ones column the 1 has a value of 1, or 1 one.

Next, subtract the digits in the tens column.
2 - 1 = 1

1 ten + 1 one = 11
There are 11 bears total.

With extra teddies in tow,
let's subtract some more.

17
− 11
—
6

Trying new equations
is what math is for.

$$30 - 10 = 20$$

Sometimes you must borrow.

Don't worry or fret.

1. The number 37 is larger than the number 19. But in the ones column, the larger number is on the bottom. To subtract, you must borrow a 10 from the tens column. Now there are only 2 tens left in the tens column.

2. The 7 becomes a 17.

3. Subtract in the ones column. 17 ones minus 9 ones equals 8 ones.

4. Subtract in the tens column. 2 tens minus 1 ten equals 1 ten.

5. Add to find the difference. 1 ten plus 8 ones equals 18. The difference is 18.

Go from many to few.

Let's see what you get.

First, borrow a ten from the tens column.

2   17

37

Second, add the ten to the ones column.

−19

Third, subtract the numbers in the ones column.
17 − 9 = 8

Fourth, subtract the numbers in the tens column.
2 − 1 = 1

18

18 teddies are left!

CRAYON

We'll try it again
and borrow this time, too.
Take the bottom from the top—
you know just what to do.

$$\begin{array}{r} 41 \\ -17 \\ \hline \end{array}$$

First, borrow a ten from the tens column.

$$\overset{3}{4}\overset{11}{1}$$

Second, add the ten to the ones column.

$$-17$$

Third, subtract the numbers in the ones column.
11 – 7 = 4

Fourth, subtract the numbers in the tens column.
3 – 1 = 2

24

24 teddies are left!

Now we must celebrate, for you are most skilled!
You've mastered subtraction, and the teddies are thrilled.

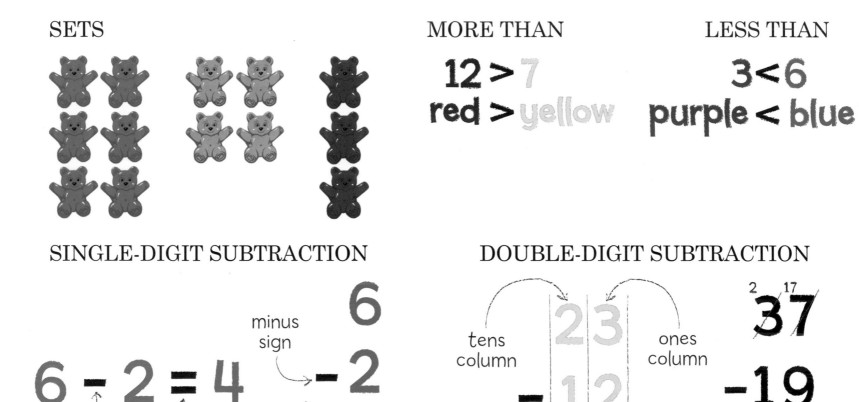

SETS

MORE THAN

12 > 7
red > yellow

LESS THAN

3 < 6
purple < blue

SINGLE-DIGIT SUBTRACTION

6 - 2 = 4

minus sign
equal sign

6
- 2
4

minus sign

DOUBLE-DIGIT SUBTRACTION

tens column

ones column

- 23
12
11

2 17
37
-19
18